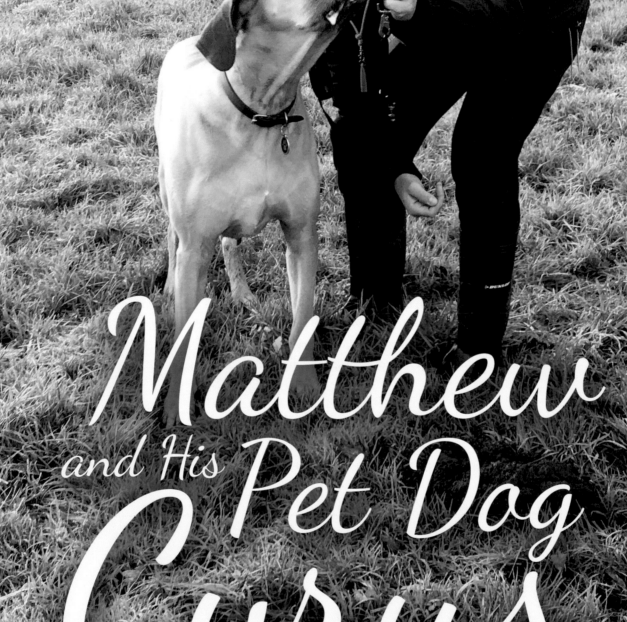

James Taylor

Matthew
and His Pet Dog
Cyrus

To order additional copies of this book, contact:
Xlibris
UK TFN: 0800 0148620 (Toll Free inside the UK)
UK Local: 02036 956328 (+44 20 3695 6328 from outside the UK)
www.xlibrispublishing.co.uk
Orders@ Xlibrispublishing.co.uk

ISBN: 978-1-6641-1209-4 (sc)
ISBN: 978-1-6641-1210-0 (e)

Print information available on the last page

Rev. date: 07/23/2020

Matthew and His Pet Dog Cyrus

One sunny Saturday morning Matthew had woken up feeling excited as he knew that it was that time of the day where he gets to take his best friend and pet dog Cyrus out for his morning walk.

It was 08:30 in the morning and Matthew had rushed down the stairs to see his best friend Cyrus. Cyrus was a very big Great Dane that was a lovely light brown colour and everyone loved Cyrus.

Come on then Cyrus let's get ready and go for our morning walk said Matthew. Cyrus got off his bed wagging his tail jumping about excited to go for his morning walk with Matthew.

Matthew had got Cyrus's treat's in his pocket and then took Cyrus out to the car so they could drive to their favourite place to walk.

As Matthew and Cyrus turned up to their favourite place to walk (Ashton Court) Cyrus jumped up barking wagging his tail looking at Matthew as Cyrus wanted to get out of the car and start his morning walk.

Matthew and Cyrus had left the car and started to walk towards the field, Cyrus was so happy that he was going to be able to play in this field.

Matthew had opened the big black gate and Cyrus ran in to the field so happy and full of life, wanting Matthew to throw Cyrus's toy for him.

Matthew got out Cyrus's squeaky toy that looked like a bone, but it had a black and white print on it like it was a football and squeak's very loud.

Cyrus started to run around in a circle with excitement because he had seen that Matthew had brought Cyrus's favourite toy. Matthew looked at Cyrus and said 'Ready Steady Go' and throw the bone for Cyrus.

Cyrus went running after his bone, galloping like a horse as he was such a big dog. 'Come on Cyrus' shouted Matthew, bring your bone back here and Cyrus did over and over again as Matthew and Cyrus were having so much fun together.

Matthew picked up Cyrus's bone and said to Cyrus there's and big pond over there, let's go over there so you can have a drink of water to cool you down Cyrus.

After Cyrus had had a drink of the pond water, Matthew had an idea of talking Cyrus for a walk up throw the wood's as Cyrus needed to have a good run about to burn some of that Great Dane energy that Cyrus has.

So, Matthew and Cyrus started to walk in the woods. Cyrus started to look around, sniffing and barking. Matthew was thinking to himself "Cyrus what's wrong".

Matthew then could see that Cyrus was looking at the top of the hill in the wood's where Cyrus could see his friend Poppy.

Poppy was a beautiful black and white German Shepard who Cyrus love to chase and run around with, As Cyrus and Poppy were best friends.

Matthew said to Cyrus "Go on then Cyrus go see Poppy". Cyrus went running off up to the top of the hill in the woods to see.

Cyrus and Poppy had started to run around barking, chasing one another around the field. When Matthew had got to the top of the hill, he could see Cyrus and poppy, but couldn't see Poppy's owner Lyn.

Matthew called out to Cyrus and Poppy "Come one you two let's go and find Lyn "and they had started to walk down the big hill leading out of the woods in to the big open space, where in that field there was some many other people with their dog's all running about. Cyrus and Poppy was very excited to see this and went running off to see if they knew any of the other dog's that are running around in the big field.

As Matthew had got down to the bottom of the hill, he had seen Lyn calling out "Poppy come here Poppy where are you". Matthew shouted out to Lyn "its ok Lyn Poppy is running around the field with Cyrus, we spotted her on the top of the hill in the wood's.

Lyn had gone running up to Matthew and put her arms around him and gave him a big cuddle. Matthew said Lyn, I've been so worried, I could find poppy for age's were was she?

Matthew replied "Cyrus and I had been walking in the woods and Cyrus had seen poppy at the top of the hill". Lyn took a big breath and said to Matthew "thank you for keeping Poppy with you, she keeps running off into the woods and I get worried I wouldn't be able to find here again".

Matthew and Lyn then carried on with their walk together and Cyrus and Poppy had come back to Matthew and Lyn and started to walk along side on another.

As Matthew and Lyn continued walking talking about their family's and how they are doing, Cyrus and Poppy had been sniffing around and found a stick that they then started to both tug on.

Matthew and Cyrus were nearly at the end of their walk, and you could see that Cyrus and Poppy was not yet ready to leave, but it was time to go home.

Matthew and Lyn had both said good bye and see you again some time. Cyrus and Poppy had then been put on their leads and Matthew and Lyn had gone their own sperate way's.

Matthew had said to Cyrus "Come on then Cyrus, Let's go home and have some breakfast'. After Matthew and Cyrus had had breakfast, Matthew could see that Cyrus wasn't happy. This could have been due to Cyrus was missing Poppy.

Matthew had an Idea, Matthew had said to his mum and dad, where is James as Cyrus doesn't seem happy so I think James and I should give Cyrus a bath in the back garden and then after he is dry and relaxed for some time, we could play some game's with Cyrus.

James had come down stairs and said to Matthew, did you and Cyrus enjoy your walk. I would have come with you but I over slept…

Matthew had said to James on what the walk was like that what happened with Lyn and Poppy. James was glade that Lyn had got poppy back ok and that Matthew managed to spend some time with Lyn before coming home.

James said to Matthew, if Cyrus doesn't look to happy then let's give him a bath and speak to mum and dad and see what they say about inviting Lyn over for lunch and ask Lyn to bring poppy with her so that Cyrus and Poppy can play in the garden.

Matthew had spoken to his Mum and Dad (Lou and Andy) and they had both said yes lets ring Lyn and get her to come to lunch with Poppy so that Cyrus and Poppy can both play in the garden together, that would cheer Cyrus up.

So, Lou and Andy, Matthew's mum and dad had contacted Lyn, Asked Lyn to come to lunch and to bring Poppy with her so that Cyrus and Poppy can play in the garden.

Once everyone had had lunch, they had all gone out into the garden so that Cyrus and Poppy could play with one another.

Matthew and James had been throwing ball's and toy's for Cyrus and Poppy to play with. You could really tell by the look on Cyrus that he was enjoying himself and the love he had for Matthew and he kept running up to Matthew licking him on the face.

Matthew and James continued to play with Cyrus and Poppy outside in the Garden throwing toys for Cyrus and Poppy until it was time that Lyn and Poppy had to go home.

After Lyn and Poppy had gone home Matthew had seen that Cyrus was trying to dig up an area in the garden, so Matthew had gone out side to see what Cyrus was trying to get.

Matthew had always thought that Cyrus was a little different from other dog's and was surprised at what Cyrus had come across when he stopped digging.

Matthew said to Cyrus "here boy what have you found there". It was an old wooden box that had something written on it but you couldn't really see what it said on the box, as the box was old dirty and damaged by the look of it.

So Matthew had taken the box into his mum and dad to show them what Cyrus had dug up. Matthew's mum and dad had never seen the box before and didn't know where or who had put it there. Cyrus was looking really please with himself.

Matthew had managed to open the box in front of his mum dad James and Cyrus to find that there was a note left in the box with a old photo and what looked to be a dog tag with a name on it. The name on the dog tag was Patch and the photo was of an old lady with her dog sat on her lap in the garden. The garden in the photo was the garden that belongs to Matthew's mum and dad.

Matthew asked his parent's if they knew of the lady and the dog in the photo, both his mum and dad told Matthew that they didn't know the lady in the photo either the dog. Everyone was very confused.

The letter left by the old lay in the photo had said;

Dear new owner,

My name is Nanny Higs. I have lived here all my life. I got married to my husband frank 32 years ago and he passed away in 1989. I am writing you this letter to say that there have been some very good memories in the house and that is all down to me always having a pet dog. I have found that every time I have a pet dog my life is complete and that I just wanted to show you in this photo that I have left how happy I was and to ensure that you never go without having a pet dog. I hope that you all are well and enjoying your life in this house.

Your sincerely

Nanny Higs

Matthew and his mum dad and James become confused on why Nanny Higs stated in the letter that you need to make sure that you are never without a pet dog in the house, and they carried on with their day to day life.

During the rest of the afternoon Matthew and James had seen that Cyrus was acting a little funny and couldn't work out why this was. They had both sat on the floor smoothing and talking to Cyrus, giving him lots of love and treat yet Cyrus was just not right. At about 19:00 James had said to Matthew that he was going to have a shower.

Matthew had continued to carry on watching a film on the tv when he felt a shiver of coldness. Cyrus was looking at the lounge door, but nobody was there, yet Matthew felt very cold and Cyrus was barking and barking at what looked like to be nothing.

As Matthew had paused the film on tv he heard this little whisper that sounded like an old lady say; *There is no need to be afraid I just wanted to say I can see how happy you and Cyrus are and that you are both very good friends, please don't ever give up on this and remember there are plenty of my items to find around the house, love Nanny Hig's.*

With that Cyrus stops barking but Matthew shouted for his mum and dad and as well as James.

Matthews mum and dad come running up he stairs to find out what all the shouting was about. James come out of the bathroom with his pjs on and wanted to know what has happened.

Matthew had told them all what Cyrus was like before it happened and what he heard an old lady say. Matthews mum and dad said that it was something that was just playing on your mind and try to forget about it. However, James was thinking something else as James could see by the look on Matthews face that something had happened.

James said to Matthew did that really happen as when I was in the shower there was a sound as if it was a dog that wanted to play, and I thought that Cyrus was wanting to play with one of his toys with you Matthew.

Matthew and James carried on watching the film on tv as Cyrus settled and fell asleep on his large dog bed under the tv that's on the wall.

A few weeks had passed and neither Matthew, James or Cyrus had found anything else that was left from the old lady, neither did they hear the old lady's voice or the sound of the dog barking again.

One day six months later Matthew Cyrus James and Matthews mum and dad had all gone to Devon for a weekend break in their caravan. Matthew and James had gone for a walk along the beach, Matthew had stated to James that they should have taken Cyrus with them as Cyrus would have really enjoyed it on the beach.

Matthew and James said that they were going to go and get a few thing's from the shop and go back to the caravan to spend some time with Matthew's mum and dad and most of all Cyrus Matthews best friend.

When Matthew and James had got back to the caravan, they could see that there was a little note on the caravan door. The note stated to *always love your family and that you will never lose your best friend as they are family to*. Matthew and James thought that Matthews mum and dad was playing a game with them and left that note there thinking that Matthew and James would believe it.

Matthew and James had gone into the caravan and said to Matthews mum and dad "Haha that was very funny leaving that note outside, but we know it was you'.

Matthews mum and dad had said "what note, we haven't left you a note as we are here in the caravan, why would we leave you that note?'. Matthews mum and dad could see that they looked worried and asked to see the note that was left on the caravan door.

Matthews mum and dad said "that looks like the handwriting of the letter that was in the box from the back garden. Everyone looked puzzled.

They had all continued with the Holiday, going to the beach, out walking to different plays, taking lots of photos and most of all taking Cyrus with them all as a family.

It had come t the time where everyone had to go home. When Matthew and the family got back to Bristol there was a note found in the lounge upstirs. The note had said *"I could see you all enjoying yourself as a family and that you could tell that Cyrus was enjoying the family time as well"*.

This had really scared Matthew but didn't want to say anything to his mum or dad but did show James the letter. James really don't know what to say or how to react.

James said to Matthew maybe we should have a look on the Internet to see if we can find any background of the lady in the photo. Matthew Stated that sounds a good idea I will get on and do that right away.

After an hour or two Matthew couldn't find any information on the old lady that used to live in there house anywhere.

So we took each day as it came looking searching for more information about this lady that left the box with the note, the photo and the dog tag in the garden.

As the time had gone on we all felt a lot closer, not that we wasn't at first just that the feeling that the box was put there for a reason and that for some reason we felt more safe.

Cyrus was Cyrus a loving cuddly warm Great Dane, Matthew was out working, Cyrus didn't like that as he would miss Matthew, James continued to work and mum and dad spent their time at home as they are both retired so that was company for both Cyrus and Matthews parents.

Weeks had passed and there wasn't anything else that we could find out about this lady who left the box, and no other letters found or anything.

In the end we had come to think that nothing would ever come of this box and life would just keep going on as it was.

As nothing had come of this, we as a family decided to lock the box away and leave it as it would be a shame to throw something like that away.

A few months later Lyn had come to lunch again and brought Poppy with her. Cyrus was full of life and was so happy to see Lyn and Poppy.

Cyrus and Poppy started to play in the garden once again with one another, And Matthew and James joined in, it was such a great afternoon. We were all having so much fun.

Cyrus had then picked up a sent and started to dig in the part of the garden where he had dug the box up from, to find that the box was back there.

We all felt very confused. There was a note, a photo of an old lady with a dog on her lap in the garden with a dog tag with patch written on it.

We think that it was a sign to say" A pet dog isn't just a pet dog. They are a family member. They feel like we feel, they love like we love and most of all they are a part of your family.

A year later and still no other signs had come to light. Matthew, Cyrus and the family continued with their life's. Matthew and Cyrus continued to go on their fun filled walks, and James joined them at times.

Printed in the United States
By Bookmasters